SCHOLASTIC

READ & RESPOND

Bringing the best books to life in the classroom

Activities based on Poppy Field

By Michael Morpurgo

MICHAEL MORPURGO
POPPY FIELD

Illustrated by
MICHAEL FOREMAN

FOR AGES 7–11

Published in the UK by Scholastic Education, 2019
Book End, Range Road, Witney, Oxfordshire, OX29 0YD
A division of Scholastic Limited
London – New York – Toronto – Sydney - Auckland
Mexico City – New Delhi – Hong Kong

SCHOLASTIC and associated logos are trademarks and/or registered trademarks of Scholastic Inc.

Printed and bound by Ashford Colour Press
© 2019 Scholastic Ltd
1 2 3 4 5 6 7 8 9 9 0 1 2 3 4 5 6 7 8

British Library Cataloguing-in-Publication Data
A catalogue record for this book is available from the British Library.
ISBN 978-1407-18323-7

Extracts from *The National Curriculum in England, English Programme of Study* © Crown Copyright. Reproduced under the terms of the Open Government Licence (OGL). http://www.nationalarchives.gov.uk/doc/open-government-licence/version/3

Author Jillian Powell
Editorial team Rachel Morgan, Vicki Yates, Suzanne Adams, Julia Roberts
Series designer Dipa Mistry
Typesetter QBS Learning
Illustrator Michael Foreman

Acknowledgements
The publishers gratefully acknowledge permission to reproduce the following copyright material:
David Higham Associates for permission to use the extract text written by Michael Morpurgo. Scholastic Children's Books for permission to use the cover and illustrations from Poppy Field written by Michael Morpurgo (Scholastic Children's Books, 2018). Reproduced with permission of Scholastic Children's Books. All rights reserved.

Every effort has been made to trace copyright holders for the works reproduced in this book, and the publishers apologise for any inadvertent omissions.

How to use Read & Respond in your classroom...

Read & Respond provides teaching ideas related to a specific well-loved children's book. Each Read & Respond book is divided into the following sections:

ABOUT THE BOOK AND AUTHOR

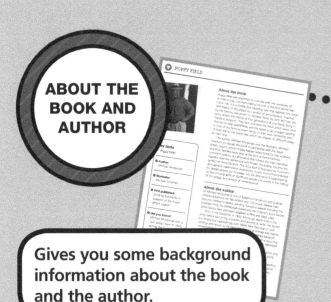

Gives you some background information about the book and the author.

GUIDED READING

Breaks the book down into sections and gives notes for using it with guided reading groups. A bookmark has been provided on page 12 containing comprehension questions. The children can be directed to refer to these as they read.

SHARED READING

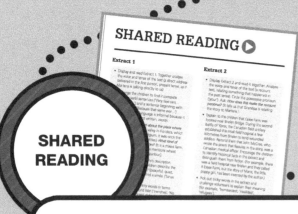

Provides extracts from the children's book with associated notes for focused work. There is also one non-fiction extract that relates to the children's book.

GRAMMAR, PUNCTUATION & SPELLING

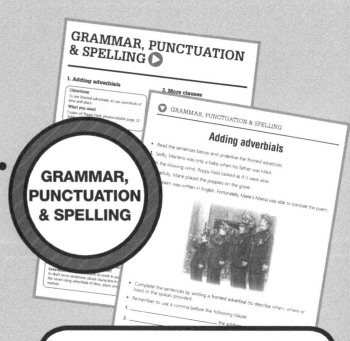

Provides word-level work related to the children's book so you can teach grammar, punctuation and spelling in context.

PLOT, CHARACTER & SETTING

Contains activity ideas focused on the plot, characters and the setting of the story.

GET WRITING

Provides writing activities related to the children's book. These activities may be based directly on the children's book or be broadly based on the themes and concepts of the story.

TALK ABOUT IT

Has speaking and listening activities related to the children's book. These activities may be based directly on the children's book or be broadly based on the themes and concepts of the story.

ASSESSMENT

Contains short activities that will help you assess whether the children have understood concepts and curriculum objectives. They are designed to be informal activities to feed into your planning.

❝ The titles are great fun to use and cover exactly the range of books that children most want to read. It makes it easy to explore texts fully and ensure the children want to keep on reading more. ❞

Chris Flanagan, Year 5 Teacher, St Thomas of Canterbury Primary School

Activities

The activities follow the same format:

• **Objective:** the objective for the lesson. It will be based upon a curriculum objective, but will often be more specific to the focus being covered.

• **What you need:** a list of resources you need to teach the lesson, including photocopiable pages.

• **What to do:** the activity notes.

• **Differentiation:** this is provided where specific and useful differentiation advice can be given to support and/or extend the learning in the activity. Differentiation by providing additional adult support has not been included as this will be at a teacher's discretion based upon specific children's needs and ability, as well as the availability of support.

The activities are numbered for reference within each section and should move through the text sequentially – so you can use the lesson while you are reading the book. Once you have read the book, most of the activities can be used in any order you wish.

CURRICULUM LINKS

Section	Activity	Curriculum objectives
Guided reading		Comprehension: To explain and discuss their understanding of what they have read. (Y5/6)
Shared reading	1	Comprehension: To discuss and evaluate how authors use language, including figurative language. (Y5/6)
	2	Comprehension: To discuss their understanding and explore the meaning of words in context. (Y5/6)
	3	Comprehension: To identify how language, structure and presentation contribute to meaning. (Y5/6)
	4	Comprehension: To check that the text makes sense to them, discussing their understanding and the meaning of words in context. (Y3/4)
Grammar, punctuation and spelling	1	Vocabulary, grammar and punctuation: To use fronted adverbials. (Y3/4) To use adverbials of time and place (Appendix 2). (Y5)
	2	Vocabulary, grammar and punctuation: To extend the range of sentences with more than one clause by using a wider range of conjunctions including when, if, because, although. (Y3/4)
	3	Vocabulary, grammar and punctuation: To use and punctuate direct speech. (Y3/4)
	4	Transcription: To spell further homophones. (Y3/4)
	5	Vocabulary, grammar and punctuation: To use passive verbs to affect the presentation of information in a sentence. (Y5/6) To choose pronouns appropriately for clarity and cohesion and to avoid repetition. (Y3/4)
	6	Vocabulary, grammar and punctuation: To use expanded noun phrases to convey complicated information concisely. (Y5/6)
Plot, character and setting	1	Comprehension: To identify how language structure and presentation contributes to meaning. (Y3–6) To summarise the main ideas drawn from more than one paragraph. (Y5/6)
	2	Spoken language: To give well-structured explanations and narratives. (All years)
	3	Comprehension: To draw inferences… justifying inferences with evidence. (Y3–6)
	4	Comprehension: To understand what they read by identifying main ideas drawn from more than one paragraph and summarising these. (Y3/4)
	5	Comprehension: To ask questions to improve their understanding. (Y5/6)
	6	Comprehension: To predict what might happen from details stated and implied. (Y3–6)
	7	Comprehension: To explain and discuss their understanding of what they have read. (Y5/6)
	8	Spoken language: To use spoken language to develop understanding through speculating, hypothesising, imagining and exploring ideas. (All years)

Section	Activity	Curriculum objectives
Talk about it	1	Spoken language: To use spoken language to develop understanding through speculating. (All years)
	2	Spoken language: To consider and evaluate different viewpoints, attending to and building on the contributions of others. (All years)
	3	Spoken language: To participate in discussions and presentations. (All years)
	4	Spoken language: To use spoken language to develop understanding through exploring ideas. (All years)
	5	Spoken language: To give well-structured descriptions, explanations and narratives for different purposes, including for expressing feelings. (All years)
	6	Spoken language: To articulate and justify answers, arguments and opinions. (All years)
Get writing	1	Composition: To use similar writing as models for their own. (Y5/6)
	2	Composition: To draft and write by composing and rehearsing sentences orally (including dialogue). (Y3/4)
	3	Composition: To perform their own compositions, using appropriate intonation, volume and movement so that meaning is clear. (Y5/6)
	4	Composition: To select the appropriate form and use similar writing as models for their own. (Y5/6)
	5	Composition: To note and develop initial ideas, drawing on reading and research where necessary. (Y5/6)
	6	Transcription: To use dictionaries to check the spelling and meaning of words; to investigate spelling and understand the spelling of some words needs to be learned specifically. (Y5/6)
Assessment	1	Vocabulary, grammar and punctuation: To use and punctuate direct speech. (Y3/4)
	2	Comprehension: To summarise the main ideas drawn from more than one paragraph. (Y5/6) To identify themes. (Y3/4)
	3	Spoken language: To give well-structured descriptions, explanations and narratives for different purposes, including for expressing feelings. (All years)
	4	Composition: To note and develop initial ideas, drawing on reading and research where necessary. (Y5/6)
	5	Composition: To select the appropriate form and use similar writing as models for their own. (Y5/6)
	6	Transcription: To investigate spelling and understand the spelling of some words needs to be learned specifically. (Y5/6) Spoken language: To use relevant strategies to build their vocabulary.(All years)

Key facts

Poppy Field

◉ **Author:**
Michael Morpurgo

◉ **Illustrator:**
Michael Foreman

◉ **First published:**
2018 by Scholastic in
support of the Royal
British Legion

◉ **Did you know?**
Michael Morpurgo was a
'war baby', born in 1943,
during the Second World
War.

About the book

Poppy Field was published to coincide with the centenary of Armistice Day, commemorating the end of the First World War (1914–18). It is a simple, but haunting, tale that explores the origin and legacy of the poppy as a symbol of remembrance. Inspired by the famous war poem 'In Flanders Fields' by John McCrae, the story relates the history of four generations of one family living in Flanders, Belgium. They farm and tend the fields which were once First World War battlefields, and the faded scrap of paper bearing a verse of the famous poem hangs on their wall, reminding them of their link to the Great War which has shaped, in different ways, all their lives.

The author, Michael Morpurgo, and the illustrator, Michael Foreman, produced the book in partnership with the Royal British Legion, whose Poppy Appeal raises funds for war veterans and their families every year at the time of Remembrance commemorations. An afterword that follows the main narrative explains how the ephemeral wild flower, the poppy, became the symbol of remembrance. The story itself is illustrated by Foreman's atmospheric watercolour illustrations, mostly monochrome except for details picked out in poppy red; the afterword is supported by archive photographs of significant people and events in the history of the poppy as a symbol of remembrance.

About the author

Sir Michael Morpurgo is one of Britain's most famous and popular children's authors. He has written over 100 novels. Several have become children's classics, winning numerous awards including the Smarties Prize, the Whitbread Award and the Children's Book Award. Some books have also been adapted as films and stage plays.

Born in Hertfordshire in 1943, Morpurgo spent time in the army before becoming a teacher and starting to write. His stories are simply but captivatingly told. Many have historical or rural settings and return to his favourite themes of animals and nature, environmental issues and barrier-breaking friendships between humans and animals or old and young. War has been a recurring theme in his novels including *The Butterfly Lion* (1996), *Warhorse* (1982) and *Private Peaceful* (2003).

Morpurgo was the Children's Laureate from 2003 to 2005 and has won many honours including an MBE, an OBE and, in 2018, a knighthood for his services to literature and charity.

He continues to write novels, screenplays and libretti, travelling all over the United Kingdom and abroad addressing audiences at literary festivals, telling his stories and explaining the inspiration behind them, and encouraging us all to record and tell our own stories.

GUIDED READING ▶

Cover and verse

Introduce the book by examining the cover together, looking for clues to the content and setting (rural/farm setting, First World War soldier, connection to the Royal British Legion Poppy Appeal). Ask the children if they can explain the connection between poppies and war. (Before and on Remembrance Sunday each November, many people wear a poppy as a symbol of remembrance of those who lost their lives in war. The Royal British Legion Poppy Appeal raises funds by selling poppies to support veterans and their families.) Note the 'thank you' that prefaces the story and encourage a volunteer to explain why and to whom we should feel gratitude (to those who died in war, sacrificing their own lives for the future of others).

Read the verse of John McCrae's poem, 'In Flanders Fields' on the page before the story starts. Tell the children that this is the first verse of a famous poem by the war poet John McCrae. Pause to reflect on the words, considering who is speaking and what has happened to them (soldiers who have died in the war and are now buried in the fields of Flanders). Encourage the children to use the illustration to interpret the words and suggest that they should continue to do this throughout the novel.

Martens's introduction

Turn the page and read the first paragraphs as far as 'That's 87 years after the war ended.' Review what we learn from these first paragraphs. Ask: *Who is the narrator?* (a boy called Martens Merkel) *Where does he live?* (on a farm in Flanders) Establish some key facts about the First World War. (It was fought between Britain and her allies against Germany and her allies; it lasted for four years, from 1914 to 1918,

and the battlegrounds were in France and Flanders, now a province of northern Belgium.) Note the term 'trenches', asking if any of the children can explain the meaning. (During the First World War, the enemy armies fought from a network of long, narrow ditches dug into the ground.) Discuss the war graves and ask the children if any of them have visited the memorials or cemeteries, or have relatives who have visited them or are in some way connected with the First World War. Tell them that it was also called the 'Great War' and the 'war to end all wars' because so many lives (over 16 million) were lost in terrible warfare. Ask: *What question is raised about the death of Martens's father?* (Martens says the war killed him, but not until 2005, 87 years after the war ended.)

Read the next paragraph and ask a volunteer to explain what happened to Martens's father. (He was killed by an unexploded shell, a type of bomb.) Continue reading as far as 'the story he used to tell Papa when he was my age'. Ask: *What can we now predict about the narrative that follows?* (It is going to be Grandpa's story, the family story.) Carry on reading as far as Grandpa's words 'You look out across the whole farm from there'. Pause to reflect how time has changed the landscape: once it was a terrible battlefield, now it is peaceful farmland again. Continue reading to the break in the text ('but how I remember him telling it.')

Explore what we learn about the poem generally, and also its significance to the family. (It is a famous poem; it hangs in the hallway of their house and they regard it as a lucky talisman.) Ask: *Why do you think the writing is 'full of corrections and crossings out'?* (It was the poet's first draft, when he was still composing it and so was revising words and phrases.)

The beginning of Grandpa's story

Note that after the text break the narrative voice shifts from Martens to his grandfather, as the old man begins telling the family story. Raise questions 11 and 13 on the Guided reading bookmark. Read as far as 'And here's why'. Consider question 9 on the bookmark. Pick out key words and phrases, explaining their meaning in the context of the war ('Ypres', 'Tommies', 'bombarded'). Note the spelling and pronunciation of Ypres (tell the children that the British soldiers pronounced it 'Wipers' because they were not familiar with the French pronunciation). Raise question 10 on the bookmark and encourage children to look out for further examples as they read. Ask them if they can explain what they understand by a 'field hospital' (a temporary hospital set up near the battlefield to treat injured soldiers). Encourage reference to the illustrations, noting the damaged buildings and the tent erected to provide shelter for casualties.

Marie meets the poet

Continue reading as far as 'We just buried him.' Ask the children: *Who is the soldier who speaks to Marie?* (John McCrae). Pause to explain that John McCrae was a Canadian Lieutenant-Colonel in the war. Tell the children that he was inspired to write his most famous poem, 'In Flanders Fields', in May 1915 when he saw poppies growing on the fresh grave of his friend and fellow soldier, Lieutenant Alexis Helmer, who died in the second battle of Ypres. According to one story, his fellow soldiers retrieved the poem after McCrae, who was not happy with his work, threw it away. Reflect how the author has taken historical facts and beliefs about the origins of the poem to adapt and interpret for his own story, linking to question 15 on the bookmark. In Morpurgo's story, it is Martens's great-grandmother, Marie, who lays poppies on the grave, after recovering the first draft of his poem.

Continue reading as far as 'And survive they did.' Tell the children that the poem 'In Flanders Fields' was first published in a magazine called *Punch* in London in 1915. It became very popular and verses from it were used in appeals to recruit soldiers and to raise money by selling war bonds (to raise funds for the war). The references the poem made to the red poppies that grew over the graves of fallen soldiers led to the poppy becoming a symbol of remembrance of those who have died in conflict. Review question 1 on the bookmark. Ask: *In this story, how does the author create a link between the poppy and remembrance?* (The poet asks Marie to put poppies on the grave of his dead friend). Consider the word 'talisman', checking that the children understand its meaning (something that has magic powers to bring good luck).

Martens's great-grandparents meet

Read the next two paragraphs, pausing to note how the narrator, Martens's grandfather, indicates that the story is about to move on. Ask: *Can you explain why without the 'next strange meeting' neither he nor Martens would be there?* (It is after Marie meets and marries Piet that Grandpa is born, and then his own son, Emile, and his grandson, Martens.)

Read on as far as 'So much needs healing.' Ask a volunteer to explain how the poem becomes significant in the family story for a second time. (It leads to the meeting between Marie and Piet because they both know and love the words.) Pause to ask why Marie feels the poem is 'the same but different'. (The poet will have revised and improved the poem from the first draft which Marie retrieved from the puddle.) Reflect on the idea of the land needing healing after the ravages of war, noting the contrast brought out in the illustrations that show its past and present. Raise question 3 on the bookmark.

A second war

Read the next paragraph and pause to remind the children of the dates of the Second World War (1939 to 1945). Ask: *What can we infer happened to Flanders in that war from the last sentence in the paragraph?* (The country was invaded and occupied by enemy troops.) Read on as far as 'It was our place.' *What does the illustration showing Emile as a boy suggest?* (That the poppy field had become a happy place again.) Discuss together question 8 on the bookmark. Continue reading as far as 'and simply listen in wonder.' Ask the children to summarise what Kate discovers about the poem and the poppy field. (The scrap of paper was written by the poet John McCrae and on their poppy field the enemy soldiers had joined in a Christmas truce.) Consider question 2 on the bookmark.

Ending

Read on as far as 'ten million or more', pausing to note how the story moves on to the next generation with the birth of Martens. Ask the children if they can explain what it is that Emile sees. (He has a ghostly vision of the Christmas truce between the enemy soldiers). Check that they understand the meaning of the word 'truce' (an agreement to stop fighting for a while). Ask: *What do you understand by 'No Man's Land'?* (It was the land which lay between the front lines of the enemy armies.) *Can you recall how Martens's father, Emile, becomes a casualty of the war?* (He is killed by an unexploded shell in the field.) Pause to note how the poppies are seen as symbolic of the millions of soldiers who fell in battle.

Read the last paragraphs, asking how the narrative voice shifts again (back to Martens). Raise question 6 and review question 10 on the bookmark. Ask: *What does Martens plan to do?* (go to Poppy Field, in the hope of seeing the ghostly vision of the truce as his father once did) Ask questions 4 and 5 on the bookmark. Invite the children to explore the various threads which link the four generations in the story: the words of the poem, the poppy field, singing and music. Consider questions 12 and 14 on the bookmark.

Read together McCrae's famous poem, which follows the story, encouraging subjective responses to the poem and the story. Ask: *Do you think it is a happy or sad story, or perhaps a mixture of both?* Encourage them to support their answers with reasons. Allow time to discuss questions 7, 15 and 16 on the bookmark.

Poppy Field
by Michael Morpurgo

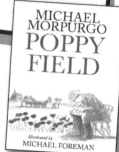

Focus on...
Meaning

1. How are poppies first used for remembrance in the story?

2. In what way is the verse of poetry significant to Martens's family?

3. What do you think the author's view of war is? Give your reasons.

Focus on...
Organisation

4. Name the family members who represent the main stages in the story.

5. Consider ways the author links the four generations of Martens's family.

6. How are Martens's words used to frame the family story?

7. How much time do you think passes during the story? Give your reasons.

8. The author uses just two sentences on one page. What effect does this have?

Poppy Field
by Michael Morpurgo

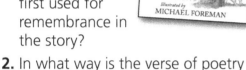

Focus on...
Language and features

9. The family story is passed down orally (spoken). How does the language reflect this?

10. Note words and terms which relate specifically to the First World War.

11. How and why does the story shift from the present to the past tense and back?

12. How do the illustrations suggest different moods in the story?

Focus on...
Purpose, viewpoints and effects

13. How does the narrative voice change and why?

14. What effect does the artist's use of the colour red have in the illustrations?

15. How does the story combine historical fact and fiction?

16. What do you think the author's main purpose was in telling this story?

SHARED READING ▶

Extract 1

- Display and read Extract 1. Together analyse the voice and tense of the text (a direct address delivered in the first person, present tense, as if Martens is talking directly to us).

- Challenge the children to find incomplete (lacking a verb) sentences ('Very few cars… Wide skies…') and a sentence beginning with a conjunction ('Because that same war…') Discuss how the language is informal because it suggests spoken, not written, words.

- Ask: *What do we learn about the place where Martens lives?* (It is in a valley in Flanders, which is part of present-day Belgium; it was once the site of First World War battles.) *What kind of farm is it? How do we know?* (It is a mixed farm; we know because Martens mentions wheat fields, cows and a milking parlour.)

- Focus on the mood Martens's description evokes. How would the children describe the place where Martens lives? (peaceful, quiet, rural) Challenge them to find a simile. ('lanes like ribbons')

- Ask the children to identify words or terms specific to the First World War ('trenches', 'No Man's Land') and suggest definitions. Ask: *What are the only signs of the war now?* (the cemeteries and memorials)

- Can the children describe what the same landscape would have been like during the war? (noisy with shelling and gunfire; muddy and covered with debris and rubble)

- Ask: *What question does the author raise in the last sentences?* (How the war killed Martens's father so long after it ended.)

Extract 2

- Display Extract 2 and read it together. Analyse the voice and tense of the text (a recount text, relating something that happened in the past tense). Circle the possessive pronoun ('your'). Ask: *How does this make the recount personal?* (It tells us that Grandpa is relating the story to Martens.)

- Explain to the children that Essex Farm was located near Brielen Bridge. During the second battle of Ypres, the Canadian field artillery established this small field hospital a few kilometres from Brielen to tend wounded soldiers. Remind them that John McCrae, who wrote the poem that features in the story, was a Canadian medical officer. Encourage the children to identify historical facts in the extract and distinguish them from fiction. (For example, there was a field hospital near Brielen and they called it Essex Farm, but the story of Marie, the little poppy girl, has been invented by the author.)

- Pick out tricky words in the extract and challenge volunteers to explain their meaning (for example, 'bombarded', 'invalided', 'refugees').

- Underline the phrase 'a matter of pride' and ask the children if they can explain what it means and then suggest a replacement. (It was important to how Marie felt about herself.) Ask: *What made Marie feel pleased and satisfied?* (when she sold all her eggs)

- Revise onomatopoeia, circling the word 'jingling' and inviting definitions (making a light metallic, clinking sound).

- Focus on the last sentence. *How does the author make us want to read on?* (We want to find out why they name Marie 'the little poppy girl'.)

Extract 3

- Display Extract 3. Underline the sentence 'It was a happy, happy day'. Ask: *Which day is Martens's grandfather describing?* (the day Martens was born) *Why does he repeat the adjective?* (for emphasis) *Can you explain the meaning of the idiom 'in good heart'?* (feeling cheerful and optimistic)

- Circle tricky words (such as 'tentatively' and 'hitch') and invite volunteers to provide meanings and suggest replacements.

- Encourage the children to explain the significance of the greatcoats – one khaki, one grey. (The British soldiers wore khaki uniforms; the Germans wore grey.)

- Ask the children: *What do you think it is that Emile sees?* (He has a vision from the past, of the Christmas truce, when soldiers came together to sing carols and exchange gifts.) *What adds to the ghostly atmosphere?* (the mist)

- Focus on the verbs, encouraging the children to note changes in tense. Scan through the text picking out the tenses and noting how the recount shifts from the past tense 'he was quiet… we knew…' to the present 'he puts on his boots… I help him…'

- Note that this is a recount text, where Grandpa describes something that happened in the past, but occasionally uses the present tense. Invite a volunteer to read aloud the sentences written in the present tense, replacing them with past-tense verbs, and encourage the children to think how this changes the effect. (The present tense suggests spoken words and gives immediacy to his memories: '(he) comes in… sits down, tells us…'.)

- Discuss the impact of the two very short sentences at the end.

Extract 4

- Read Extract 4. Discuss any facts or ideas that echo the story of *Poppy Field* (the poetic words written by a First World War soldier, poppies used as emblems of remembrance and to represent healing of the soil, the playing of the bugle).

- Circle or underline tricky words and phrases and ask the children to explain their meaning and suggest replacements ('centenary', 'art installation', 'inspired', 'ephemeral', 'eternal', 'proliferated', 'dormant', 'germinate', 'debris', 'resilient').

- Ask volunteers to cite any facts they have learned about poppies, noting them on the board. Circle '*papaver rhoeas*' and explain that botanists use Latin names to identify different families and species of plants. Challenge children to summarise why poppies multiply on battlefields. (Their seeds germinate easily in disturbed soil; lime deposits from battles encourage their growth.)

- Underline the present participles 'cascading', 'sweeping' and 'swirling', and ask what effect they have (they create the idea of flow and movement).

- Challenge the children to find examples of alliteration ('Rivers of red'; 'poppies proliferated'; 'speck-like seeds') and metaphor ('red sea', 'Rivers of red poppies').

- Focus on the contrast suggested by the adjectives in 'Tough and resilient, yet fragile and ephemeral'. Invite children to suggest facts contained in the extract which support these contrasting descriptions. (Poppies germinate easily and thrive even in poor soil, but their petals and stems are delicate and the flowers do not last long.) Ask: *In what way does this description fit the young soldiers who fought in the First World War?* (They were tough and strong yet they were easily injured and their lives were short.)

Extract 1

My name is Martens Merkel. I live on a farm in Flanders, with my mother and my grandfather. I go to school in Poperinge, just a few kilometres away. I cycle there if the weather isn't too bad. All around us are the battlefields of the First World War, which ended a long time ago, in 1918. You wouldn't know it was a battlefield now, that the trenches ran right through our farm, that where the cows now graze was No Man's Land.

Poppies grow here in their millions, so thick sometimes in the wheat field in the valley that you can barely see the wheat for the poppies. We all call it just "Poppy Field". So, one way or another, poppies have been part of my life, of all our lives, ever since I can remember – and before that even, as you will see.

It's very quiet here, just birdsong in the morning early and the milking parlour humming twice a day, a place of small woods and neat fields, and lanes like ribbons running through the farmland. Very few cars, very few people. Wide skies over a landscape of gentle hills and valleys, the towers and spires of Ypres in the distance.

You would only know there had ever been a war here from the cemeteries and memorials. There are dozens of them, hundreds probably. I've never counted them. We can see two of them from the house, go past them almost every day, one for British soldiers, one for Germans. Most of my friends hardly notice the cemeteries, because they're always there, part of the landscape. I notice them, but then I have good reason to. Because that same war killed my father, and that was 11 years ago, in the spring of 2005. That's 87 years after the war ended.

Extract 2

My mama, that's your great-grandmother, Martens – Marie, she was called – she was the one who found the poem. Marie was just a girl, about eight years old when the war came, the First World War that is, a long time before she met my father, your great-grandfather. Her family lived on a farm on the other side of Ypres, near a village called Brielen, not far from a field hospital – known as Essex Farm to the soldiers. "Tommies" the soldiers were always called. Many of the farming folk around Ypres and the townsfolk too, come to that, had already left. Ypres and everywhere around was in range of German guns and was often being bombarded. Half the town was in ruins already.

But Marie's family decided it was safer to stay. Her father, wounded in the war, invalided out of the Belgian army, had seen the misery of the thousands of refugees on the roads, with nowhere to go. At least if they stayed at home they could feed themselves, he thought.

Better to stay together, shelter in the cellar, sell a few eggs and chickens, some hay and straw to the Tommies. He thought they could just about manage to get by, and they did.

He would send Marie up to the Field Hospital each day with a basket of eggs to sell. She was good at it too. It was a matter of pride to her to come home each time with her money jingling in her pocket, and her basket empty. The Tommies at the Field Hospital got used to seeing her, liked to see her. "The little poppy girl", they came to call her. And here's why.

Extract 3

And this is where you come into the story, Martens, my grandson, their son. It was a happy, happy day. 'Course, you kept us awake a bit at nights, but that's what babies do. You were so small, Martens, your fingers specially, but they were strong fingers. You gripped like you'd never let go. And all was well – the farm and the family, all of us, in good heart.

And then one morning, the Christmas after you were born, your papa comes in for breakfast, sits down at the kitchen table and tells us this story, how he'd been down to Poppy Field – and that in itself was strange, he said, because he didn't even know why he had gone there. He was just drawn there. There was a mist rising all along the valley as the sun came up, he said. He had never seen a morning of such beauty. He found himself walking through this mist, when he heard voices. Then he saw them, he told us, just as surely he was seeing us, two men walking towards one another, tentatively, meeting, then standing there talking, smoking, two soldiers from the First World War in greatcoats, one khaki and one grey. He watched them for a while, saw them shaking hands, then walking away from one another. "It happened, honest to God," your papa told us, "right before my eyes."

For days afterwards he was quiet, your papa, and we knew where his thoughts were. Then he puts on his boots after breakfast one morning just a few days later, to go ploughing in Poppy Field, mist still over the valley. I help him hitch up the plough in the farmyard, your mama comes out with his thermos of coffee, and we watch him drive away on the tractor, watch him disappear into the mist. And that was it. We never saw him again.

Extract 4

Papaver Rhoeas

For a few months in 2014, the imposing, grey Tower of London was transformed by a red sea of poppies to mark the centenary of the outbreak of the First World War. The public art installation 'Blood swept lands and seas of red'

was inspired by words taken from the last will of an unknown soldier who died in Flanders. Rivers of red poppies seemed to flow from the tower, cascading from a window, sweeping over the arch of the main entrance and swirling around the moat. Each one of hundreds of thousands of ceramic poppy heads represented a soldier who had died in the First World War. They had been placed, one by one, by volunteers in remembrance of the dead, to commemorate the fallen and to raise funds for armed services charities. Millions of visitors flocked to see the moving spectacle and to hear the bugle sound the last post at sunset each day.

The corn poppy, *papaver rhoeas,* with its delicate, ephemeral petals and stems, has long been an emblem of remembrance. The ancient Greeks and Romans gave poppies as offerings to the dead and carved them on tombs as symbols of eternal sleep. It was during the Napoleonic Wars of the early 1800s that people first recorded how poppies proliferated in war zones. A single poppy flower can produce up to 60,000 speck-like seeds, which can lie dormant in the soil for up to 80 years. When the earth is disturbed, by farming, burial or warfare, these tiny, kidney-shaped seeds readily germinate even in poor, thin soil. The debris of war can also leave lime deposits in the soil which encourage their growth. After the ravages of trench warfare during the Great War, when the fields of Flanders had been churned into muddy wastelands by tanks and shelling, corn poppies bloomed in their millions. Tough and resilient, yet fragile and ephemeral, they came to symbolise the fallen soldiers as well as the healing of the land.

GRAMMAR, PUNCTUATION & SPELLING ▶

1. Adding adverbials

Objectives
To use fronted adverbials; to use adverbials of time and place.

What you need
Copies of *Poppy Field*, photocopiable page 22 'Adding adverbials'.

What to do
- Write on the board the sentence 'The soldier tore out a page from the notepad.' Invite the children to suggest some words or phrases to extend the sentence. Prompt them to think when, where or how he tore out the page, for example: 'Suddenly, the soldier tore out a page from the notepad.' (when); 'Sitting by the ambulance, the soldier tore out a page from the notepad.' (where); 'Impatiently, the soldier tore out a page from the notepad.' (how)

- Explain that adverbs, or phrases that act as adverbs (adverbials) like these, can qualify or tell us more about an action. They can even change the sense completely. Demonstrate this by writing on the board 'Angrily/Excitedly/Calmly, the soldier tore out a page from the notepad.' Point out that the adverbial is separated from the main clause that follows using a comma.

- Challenge the children to work in pairs to complete photocopiable page 22 'Adding adverbials'. Remind them to use commas as necessary.

- When they have completed the photocopiable sheet, bring the class back together to review their work.

Differentiation
Support: Provide a list of adverbs or phrases to help pairs fill in the photocopiable sheet.
Extension: Invite the children to work in pairs to draft more sentences about characters from the novel using adverbials of time, place and manner.

2. More clauses

Objective
To extend the range of sentences with more than one clause using conjunctions.

What you need
Copies of *Poppy Field*.

What to do
- Write on the board some short, factual sentences about Marie – for example: 'Marie sells eggs to the soldiers.'; 'Marie is known as the little poppy girl.'; 'Marie picks up the scrap of paper.'

- Tell the children they are going to try extending the sentences using conjunctions. Discuss some possible conjunctions or connecting words such as 'after', 'because', 'when', 'while', 'if'.

- Model some examples on the board, underlining or circling the conjunctions: 'Marie is known as the little poppy girl <u>because</u> she gives poppies away with the eggs.'; 'Marie walks up to the soldier <u>when</u> she sees him sitting by the ambulance.'; 'Marie picks up the scrap of paper <u>after</u> the soldier throws it away.'

- Together, create some more short, factual sentences about Marie and write them on the board.

- Arrange the class into pairs. Invite the pairs to extend the sentences you have modelled on the board, using conjunctions. Allow them time to write four or five sentences, then bring the class together to share sentences. Write the best sentences on the board, underlining or circling the conjunctions.

Differentiation
Support: Provide a list of conjunctions for children to use.
Extension: Challenge pairs to write more sentences. Ask each child to draft a short sentence for their writing partner to extend using conjunctions.

3. Direct or indirect?

Objective
To use and punctuate direct speech.
What you need
Copies of *Poppy Field*, Extract 3.

What to do

- Display Extract 3 from Shared reading. Remind the children that Grandpa is recounting an event that happened in the past, and what Emile told them at the time. Ask a volunteer to identify an example of direct speech in the extract and explain how they recognise it. ("It happened… right before my eyes." – the use of speech marks) Ask: *What effect does the direct speech have?* (It tells Martens word for word what his father said, which emphasises how his father truly believed what he had seen.)

- Explore together how we know that Emile said other things without Grandpa giving us his direct speech. ('One morning… your papa… tells us', 'he said', 'he told us' – giving Emile's reported speech) Highlight that as this is informal, spoken language (Grandpa is talking to Martens), Grandpa sometimes uses the present tense and sometimes the past for the reporting verbs. (Refer back to the Shared reading activity.)

- Arrange the children into pairs. Challenge them to rewrite all Emile's reported speech in direct speech, using the correct verb tenses and speech marks. Model an example on the board: '"I have been down to Poppy Field," he said. "That was strange in itself."'

- When they have finished, discuss how using direct speech changes the effect.

Differentiation

Support: Perform the task as a shared activity, writing suggestions on the board.
Extension: Challenge pairs to find other examples of reported speech in the story, and rewrite them as direct speech.

4. Sounds like

Objective
To find and spell homophones.
What you need
Copies of *Poppy Field*, photocopiable page 23 'Sounds like'.

What to do

- Write on the board two sentences with gaps as shown:
  - 'Marie _____ what the soldier had written on the scrap of paper.';
  - 'The _____ poppies danced in the field.'

- Ask the children to think of a word to fill the gap in each sentence ('read'/'red') and read the complete sentences aloud. Write the words in the gaps on the board. Ask: *What do you notice about the two new words?* (They sound the same.) Note the difference in spelling and introduce or revise the word 'homophone' for words that sound the same but are spelled differently.

- Challenge the children to suggest some pairs of homophones (or write words on the board and ask the children to find their homophone) to familiarise the concept. (For example, 'past'/'passed', 'four'/'for' and so on.)

- Ask children to complete photocopiable page 23 'Sounds like'. When they have finished, invite volunteers to read the sentences they completed aloud, and challenge the class to spell each word and its homophone.

- As a shared activity, identify the different parts of speech that the homophones represent: for example, 'herd' (noun)/'heard' (past-tense verb).

Differentiation

Support: Fill the gap in one sentence as a shared activity, asking pairs to find the homophone.
Extension: Working in pairs, challenge the children to draft single sentences about topics/characters from the novel that include pairs of homophones.

5. Verb switch

Objectives

To use passive verbs to affect the presentation of information in a sentence; to choose pronouns to avoid repetition.

What you need

Copies of *Poppy Field*.

What to do

- Write on the board two sentences: 'An unexploded shell <u>killed</u> Emile.' 'Emile <u>was killed by</u> an unexploded shell.'

- Underline the active and passive verbs. Ask the children what difference the verb form makes to the sense or meaning of the sentence. (The active puts the emphasis on the shell; the passive puts the emphasis on Emile.) Challenge volunteers to suggest follow-on sentences, retaining the same subject but using a pronoun to avoid repetition. For example: '<u>An unexploded shell</u> killed Emile. <u>It</u> was buried in the soil in the poppy field.'; '<u>Emile</u> was killed by an unexploded shell. <u>He</u> was driving his tractor at the time.'

- Write two more sentences on the board: 'John McCrae wrote the poem.' 'The poem was written by John McCrae.'

- Repeat the exercise to familiarise the children with the pattern.

- Arrange the children into pairs. Tell them to choose a character. One child should write a short sentence about their character using an active verb. The other should then change that verb into the passive voice. They should take turns to repeat the task using the same character.

- When they have finished, ask volunteers to read aloud their sentences. Invite children to suggest follow-on sentences using the practised pattern.

Differentiation

Support: Provide pairs with sentences using active and passive verbs and challenge them to change the verb voice.

Extension: Let pairs draft follow-on sentences for each sentence they compose, using pronouns.

6. Neat noun phrases

Objective

To use expanded noun phrases to convey complicated information concisely.

What you need

Copies of *Poppy Field*, Extract 4, photocopiable page 24 'Neat noun phrases'.

What to do

- Display an enlarged copy of Extract 4 (Shared reading). Re-read the extract together, then circle the words 'Tower', 'spectacle' and 'seeds'. Ask the children if they can identify which part of speech they are (nouns). Examine the phrases which expand the nouns to describe them further ('the imposing, grey Tower', 'the moving spectacle', 'tiny, kidney-shaped seeds').

- Tell the children we call this kind of phrase an 'expanded noun phrase'. It is a neat, concise way of telling us more about the subject (noun).

- Challenge the children to find other expanded noun phrases in the extract, underlining or circling them ('public art installation', 'poor, thin soil' and so on).

- Arrange the children into pairs and hand out photocopiable page 24 'Neat noun phrases'. Allow them time to complete the sheet, encouraging them to check by reading the matched pairs aloud to each another.

- Bring the class back together and invite volunteers to read aloud the nouns with their correct noun phrases. Let children compare and correct their work as necessary.

- Then ask pairs to create alternative noun phrases to describe the nouns (for example, 'the great stone arch', 'a poppy-strewn grave') and share these as a whole class.

Differentiation

Support: Provide a list of adjectives to help children compose their alternative noun phrases.

Extension: Challenge the children to find other nouns in the novel and compose expanded noun phrases for them.

Adding adverbials

- Read the sentences below and underline the fronted adverbials.

1. Sadly, Martens was only a baby when his father was killed.

2. In the blowing wind, Poppy Field looked as if it were alive.

3. Carefully, Marie placed the poppies on the grave.

4. The poem was written in English. Fortunately, Marie's Mama was able to translate the poem.

- Complete the sentences by writing a fronted adverbial (to describe when, where or how) in the spaces provided.

- Remember to use a comma before the following clause.

1. _____ the soldiers exchanged greetings.

2. _____ Martens listened to his grandfather's story.

3. _____ Marie's father framed the scrap of paper.

4. _____ Piet played the bugle by the Menin gate.

5. _____ the soldiers exchanged greetings.

6. _____ Emile walked through the mist.

7. _____ the land healed.

Sounds like

- Find a word and its homophone to fill the gaps in each pair of sentences.

1. The Merkels kept a _____ of cows for milking.

Marie _____ the Tommy read out the words of the poem.

2. Marie was _____ when the war came.

The soldiers _____ the eggs that Marie sold them.

3. The Merkel family _____ that their poem had become famous.

Marie put the poppies on a _____ grave.

4. The duck pond was once a large _____ in the ground.

Martens knew the _____ history of the poem.

5. Emile saw two soldiers meeting in the _____.

Grandpa said that he _____ his wife, Kate.

6. Martens is Emile Merkel's _____.

Emile said that the _____ was coming up through the mist.

- Circle the correct homophone in each sentence

1. Marie offered the soldier a flower/flour.

2. If ever Grandpa couldn't find Emile he wood/would look in Poppy Field.

3. Grandpa and Grandma loved Poppy Field; it was their favourite place/plaice.

4. The soldiers played football on Christmas knight/night.

Neat noun phrases

- Match each phrase to a noun to compose an expanded noun phrase used in the novel.
- Draw a line between the phrase and the noun it describes. The first one has been done for you.

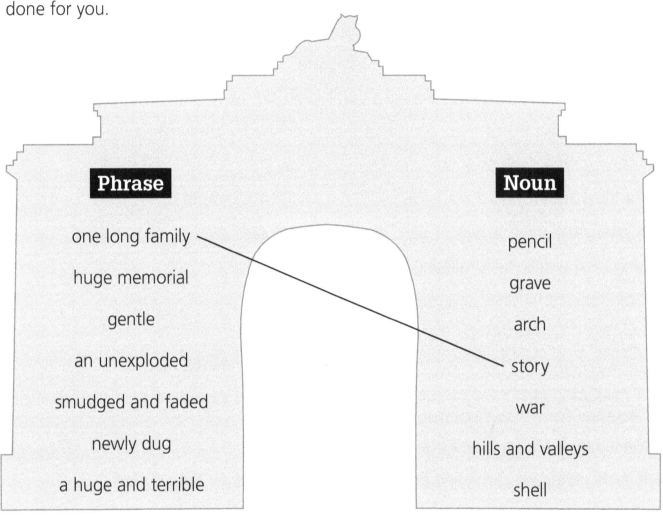

Phrase	**Noun**
one long family	pencil
huge memorial	grave
gentle	arch
an unexploded	story
smudged and faded	war
newly dug	hills and valleys
a huge and terrible	shell

- Now create alternative noun phrases to describe some of the words above.

1. _____

_____

2. _____

_____

3. _____

_____

4. _____

_____

PLOT, CHARACTER & SETTING ▶

1. Four generations

Objectives
To identify how structure contributes to meaning; to summarise the main ideas drawn from more than one paragraph.

What you need
Copies of *Poppy Field*.

Cross-curricular links
History, PSHE

What to do

- As a shared activity, construct a timeline, noting on the board in sequence the four generations of Martens's family (Marie and Piet, Grandpa and Kate, Emile and Mama, Martens).

- Ask the children if they are familiar with family trees. Encourage them to relate what they know about their own family trees. Together, use the information on the board to construct Martens's family tree, with Martens at the bottom.

- Arrange the children into small groups. Allow them time to work out roughly the time span the generations cover, scanning the text for evidence. (We learn that Marie is born in 1906 and Martens is relating the story in 2016.) Bring the class back together and share the dates, adding them next to the family tree.

- Challenge groups to skim and scan the text to find threads linking the generations in the story. They should appoint a note taker to list ideas. (For example, where they live, their work on the farm, the poem, singing/music, the poppies.)

- When they have finished, discuss their findings as a class. Note how the threads that link the generations help to structure the narrative.

Differentiation
Support: Perform the task as a shared activity.
Extension: Let groups discuss further how the shared threads feature in each generation.

2. In short

Objective
To give well-structured explanations and narratives.

What you need
Copies of *Poppy Field*.

What to do

- Tell the children that they are going to work in groups to draw up a concise summary of the story, *Poppy Field*. Suggest that we might refer to the 'narrative' rather than the 'plot' of the novel, and ask if they can explain why. (The story is presented as a true recount of a family story, with real historical events rather than as fiction.) Reflect that the story has two narrators: Martens and Grandpa. Martens's words frame the story told by his Grandpa. (Grandpa tells him the story and in turn he tells us, the readers.)

- Ask small groups to skim and scan the novel, discussing and noting key events. A note taker in each group should record these.

- When they have finished, they should use their notes to construct a concise summary of the narrative. Encourage them to use time connectives such as 'when', 'after', 'later' and so on.

- Bring the class back together and ask volunteers to read aloud their summaries. Invite comparisons between recounts, encouraging feedback and constructive criticism. Ask: *Were any key events omitted? Was the sequence clear and did the narrative flow well? How could it be improved?*

Differentiation
Support: Provide children with a timeline to help them extract the key events.
Extension: Let groups compare their summaries, deciding which are most effective and why. Can they make theirs any more concise without losing key content?

3. Martens's home

Objective
To draw inferences, justifying them with evidence.

What you need
Copies of *Poppy Field*, map showing the borders of the UK, France and Flanders in the First World War, photocopiable page 29 'Martens's home'.

Cross-curricular link
Geography

What to do

- Tell the children they are going to focus on the setting of the story: Flanders (which today is a province of northern Belgium and a small part of the Netherlands). Refer to a map to establish the areas which were the battlefields of the First World War.

- Hand out photocopiable page 29 'Martens's home' and ask children to work in pairs to complete it. They should skim and scan the story for information.

- Bring the class back together and share ideas. Encourage them to interpret clues to the landscape. For example, ask: *What do 'Wide skies' suggest?* (that the landscape is largely flat rather than mountainous, meaning you can see a long way) Explore details such as the mention of 'the Cloth Hall' (suggesting the importance of the local cloth industry).

- Discuss what helps to convey a sense of place in the novel, including the use of place names (Poperinge, Ypres, Brielen) and descriptions of the landscape.

- Encourage children to suggest their own words and phrases to describe the place where Martens lives ('rural', 'peaceful', 'countryside').

Differentiation

Support: Provide groups with page references to locate relevant information.
Extension: Challenge groups to find out more facts about the countryside in Flanders.

4. Key characters

Objective
To understand what they read by identifying main ideas drawn from more than one paragraph and summarising these.

What you need
Copies of *Poppy Field*, flash cards with names of key characters (Marie, Piet, Grandpa, Kate, Emile, Martens).

What to do

- Challenge the children to think up short, factual sentences about characters from the book. Hold up the flashcard 'Emile' and model a few examples on the board: 'Emile was Martens's father.' 'Emile was killed by an unexploded shell.'

- Arrange the children in small groups and allow them time to compose sentences. Bring the class back together and write some of the best sentences on the board, then together arrange them in a sensible order. For example: 'Emile was Martens's father. Emile was a farmer. Emile was killed by an unexploded shell.'

- Underline the repeated noun/subject and ask the children how they could use pronouns to avoid repetition (by replacing the noun 'Emile' with the pronoun 'He'). Revise the sentences on the board using pronouns appropriately: 'Emile was Martens's father. He was a farmer. He was killed by an unexploded shell.'

- Then challenge the children to find a relative pronoun to link the sentences. Provide support by listing examples on the board ('who', 'whose', 'which', 'that') and revise the sentences again: 'Emile was Martens' father. He was a farmer who was killed by an unexploded shell.'

- Repeat the exercise using the other name flash cards as prompts.

Differentiation

Support: Model sentences for each flash card before they begin.
Extension: Groups compose sentences using pronouns about characters for other groups to guess. For example: 'Every evening he plays the bugle by the Menin Gate.' (Answer: Piet)

5. Poetic links

Objective

To ask questions to improve their understanding.

What you need

Copies of *Poppy Field*, photocopiable page 30 'Poetic links'.

Cross-curricular link

History

What to do

- Tell the children they are going to focus on the way the poem 'In Flanders Fields' links several characters in the story. Revise a few facts that we know about the poem: that it was written by the Canadian Lieutenant-Colonel John McCrae; that it is a very famous First World War poem; that he wrote it after his friend died.

- Begin by asking a volunteer to summarise how, in the story, the poem is significant to the Merkel family. Remind them that Martens calls it a 'talisman'. Can they explain what that means? (It becomes like a lucky charm to them.)

- Ask the children to cite characters in the story who are linked to the poem and explain how. (For example, Marie picks up the scrap of paper; Kate learns the poem by heart and confirms who wrote it.)

- Hand out photocopiable page 30 'Poetic links' and allow the children time to complete it working in pairs.

- Bring the class back together to share findings. Encourage the children to volunteer their own thoughts and feelings about the poem. Ask: *Do you think it is a powerful war poem and if so why?*

Differentiation

Support: Establish the first link on the photocopiable page as a shared activity.

Extension: Let the children explore the afterword to learn facts about John McCrae and his famous poem.

6. Marie

Objective

To predict what might happen from details stated and implied.

What you need

Copies of *Poppy Field*.

Cross-curricular link

PSHE

What to do

- Tell the children that they are going to focus on the character of Marie. Ask a volunteer to explain her relationship to Martens (great grandmother). Together, list a few facts about her (she is eight when the war breaks out; she sells eggs at the field hospital; the soldiers call her the little poppy girl; she marries Piet).

- Arrange the children into pairs and tell them to skim and scan the story for information on Marie. They should include information about her family, her home, her daily routine and what happens to her in the story.

- Bring the class back together and share ideas. Encourage the children to think how Marie is important in the story (she brings the poem home; she lays poppies for remembrance on the grave; she marries Piet, the first generation described in the family history; they move to the farm where Martens will be born).

- Reflect on the fact that we hear no more about Marie when the story moves on to Grandpa and Kate. Encourage the children to think about her likely lifespan – she was born in 1906. Based on what we know about Marie, can they suggest what might have happened later in her life? (We know Grandpa and Kate take over the farm.)

Differentiation

Support: Provide page references to help children locate relevant information.

Extension: Let pairs develop a storyline telling what happens to Marie later in her life.

7. By chance?

Objective
To explain and discuss their understanding of what they have read.

What you need
Copies of *Poppy Field*, photocopiable page 31 'By chance?'

Cross-curricular link
PSHE

What to do
- Start by focusing on the idea of the framed poem as a 'talisman' for the Merkel family. Ask volunteers to describe how it features in the family's everyday lives: they know the words by heart, they recite it aloud and touch it for luck.

- Suggest that chance and luck, good and bad, play an important part in the storyline. Many events that happen by chance shape the family story. Arrange the children into pairs and ask them to complete photocopiable page 31 'By chance?'. Encourage them to find each event and skim and scan the story to trace its consequences (however, be aware of the potentially sensitive issue raised in the fourth event). Ask them to work together to write notes explaining the consequences. (For example: 'Marie sees the soldier throw away the paper scrap': the scrap is the famous poem which the family keep and which brings Marie and Piet together; 'Marie hears Piet read the poem at the Menin Gate': they realise they both know the words and get talking, then eventually get married and Grandpa is born.)

- When they have finished, bring the class back together to review their findings. Discuss how these events are turning points in the narrative, affecting all that follows.

Differentiation
Support: Model one or two events and their consequences on the board before they begin work.

Extension: Let pairs discuss how things would be different without each chance event happening.

8. War lives

Objective
To use spoken language to develop understanding through speculating, hypothesising, imagining and exploring ideas.

What you need
Copies of *Poppy Field*, flash cards with names of key characters (Marie, Piet, Grandpa, Kate, Emile, Mama, Martens).

Cross-curricular links
Maths, history

What to do
- Tell the children that they are going to consider how the two world wars affect the lives of characters in the novel. Arrange them into small groups and hand out flash cards (from the lesson 'Key characters') with names of characters.

- Before they begin, establish the dates of the wars, writing them on the board. (1914–18, 1939–45) Challenge the children first to work out if the character named on their card would be alive during each world war, and, if so, roughly how old they would have been.

- Explain that even if they were not alive during the war, it might have affected their life in some way, for example, its impact on their relatives or the place where they live.

- Let groups refer back to the text to find information. Encourage them to use their imaginations to speculate on how the character's life would have been affected: for example, how easy would it have been to travel? Would their food and other supplies have been affected? How would the countryside around their home have changed?

- Bring the class back together and ask volunteers from each group to summarise their findings.

Differentiation
Support: Work out characters' ages as a shared activity and provide page references to help children find information about each character.

Extension: Encourage groups to compile notes about their character and when and how their life was impacted by war.

Martens's home

• Skim and scan the story to help you complete the boxes below about Martens's home.

Describe the landscape around Poperinge.	List evidence that remains of the First World War.
What kind of farm do the Merkels own?	List any landmarks or features nearby.

Poetic links

- Choose from the characters below and match each to the correct description in the table. Write the correct name in each space.

Piet	Marie	Martens	John McCrae	Kate Moffat	Alexis Helmer

	She picks up the scrap of paper.
	She has a friend who confirms who wrote the poem.
	He writes the poem.
	The poem is a tribute to him.
	He asks Marie if he can see the framed scrap of paper.
	He knows the poem by heart.

- Write a few words to say what you think about the poem. Write about how it makes you feel.

By chance?

- These events in the story happen by chance or luck (good or bad). Explain their consequences.

Event	Explain the consequences
Marie sees the soldier throw away the paper scrap.	
Marie hears Piet read the poem at the Menin Gate.	
Grandpa and Kate meet playing music at the Menin Gate.	
Emile's tractor hits an unexploded shell.	

TALK ABOUT IT ▶

1. Remembrance

Objective

To use spoken language to develop understanding through speculating.

What you need

Copies of *Poppy Field*; images of the Menin Gate and the Cenotaph, London, Tomb of the Unknown Warrior in Westminster Abbey and/ or local war memorial/s.

Cross-curricular links

Citizenship, history

What to do

- Tell the children that they are going to explore the idea of remembrance, a key theme in the novel. Remind them how Marie's act of placing poppies on the dead soldier's grave links poppies with remembrance in the story.

- Ask a volunteer to explain what they understand by the word 'remembrance'. Ask: *What do you know about remembrance ceremonies?* Encourage them to cite national or local services or events. (For example, services in churches and by war memorials, wearing poppies, laying wreaths, bell ringing, observing silences, lighting candles.) List ideas on the board.

- View images of major war memorials. Invite the children to discuss and explain their significance (they remember and honour those who died in war and are locations for ceremonies and services to honour them). Encourage children to speculate how these memorials might offer consolation or comfort to families of the fallen (the Menin Gate records the names of soldiers with no known grave and the unknown warrior could be *any* soldier who died).

- Ask volunteers to cite local memorials and encourage children to discuss their function and purpose in their community.

Differentiation

Extension: Let children research and report on local war memorials and commemorations.

2. Why wear a poppy?

Objective

To consider and evaluate different viewpoints, attending to and building on the contributions of others.

What you need

Copies of *Poppy Field*, photocopiable page 35 'Why wear a poppy?'

Cross-curricular links

Citizenship, history

What to do

- Begin by reading through the afterword together. Pause at salient points to ask relevant questions: *Can you suggest the role and function of the British Legion?* (It is a charity that supports British service men and women, veterans and their families.) *How did John McCrae's poem first become famous?* (It was published in *Punch* in December 1915.) When you have finished reading, ask volunteers to summarise key facts and people (Moina Michael, Anna Guérin) in the history of the poppy used for remembrance. Note these on the board.

- Invite the children to discuss wearing poppies for remembrance. Tell them that the British Legion says wearing poppies is a matter of choice. They can be worn to reflect people's own thoughts and memories. Ask if any of them have seen people wearing white poppies and if they know what they represent (peace). Ask: *Why do you think some people won't wear a poppy?* (They think that this glorifies or celebrates war.) Encourage children to contribute and provide reasons for different viewpoints.

- Ask the children to work individually to complete photocopiable page 35 'Why wear a poppy?' Encourage them to find information in the afterword.

Differentiation

Extension: Let small groups of children with different viewpoints debate the wearing of poppies.

3. Poppy power

Objective
To participate in discussions and presentations.

What you need
Copies of Extract 4; images of poppy wreaths, memorials, installations; art materials.

Cross-curricular links
Citizenship, art and design

What to do

- Display Extract 4 and re-read the first paragraph. View images of the Tower of London art installation and other examples of poppies used for remembrance. (For example, poppy wreaths placed on war memorials; the poppies fluttering down at the Remembrance service in The Royal Albert Hall.) Discuss with the children the visual impact of the poppies and what they represent.

- Arrange the children into small groups. Explain that they are going to imagine they have been asked to design an art installation for remembrance using poppies. They should first choose a location: a national or local monument or landmark, or a venue such as a town hall or public park. The poppies can be made of any materials such as paper, ceramics or wool. Ask them to discuss what they want their installation to represent and what effect they hope it would have on visitors.

- Allow groups time to discuss and plan their installation. Provide them with art materials and let them together draw and annotate designs to develop their ideas.

- Ask each group to present their ideas to the class and invite children to decide which would be the most effective installations.

Differentiation

Support: Provide a simple outline of a memorial or landmark and challenge children to design an installation for it.
Extension: Let groups develop their ideas for online presentations using computer skills.

4. The Christmas truce

Objective
To use spoken language to develop understanding through exploring ideas.

What you need
Copies of *Poppy Field*.

Cross-curricular links
PSHE, history

What to do

- Tell the children they are going to focus on the Christmas truce, which features in the story. Explain that the description is based on a real event: on Christmas night of 1914, soldiers from the enemy British and German armies crossed No Man's Land to exchange gifts and greetings, play football and sing carols. Re-read the relevant passage in the story. Ask: *How do the Merkels remember and honour it?* (by singing carols each Christmas night where it happened) Invite the children to consider what the truce symbolises (friendship, hope, peace, healing).

- Then look together at Emile's ghostly vision of two soldiers greeting in the mist towards the end of the story. Ask: *How do we know that the soldiers are from opposing armies?* (by the colour of their coats)

- Ask the children to discuss what the vision signifies in the story. Ask: *Do you think it is by chance that Emile witnesses this vision? Explain why.* Encourage them to cite evidence from the text. (He says he was 'drawn' there.) Ask: *What do you think the vision represents to his family?* (It could be a sad foreshadowing of Emile's death or a reminder of a hopeful moment during the war.) Ask: *Do you think Martens will see the vision himself one day?* Encourage all children to share their opinions.

Differentiation

Support: Read the relevant passages together before discussion.
Extension: Ask small groups to research more information about the Christmas truce of 1914.

5. Stories and talismans

Objective
To give well-structured descriptions, explanations and narratives for different purposes, including for expressing feelings.

What you need
Copies of *Poppy Field*, photocopiable page 36 'Stories and talismans'.

Cross-curricular link
PSHE

What to do

- Focus on the idea of the story as a recount of a family history told by Grandpa to Martens, and in turn relayed by Martens to us, the readers. Refer to earlier work ('Poetic links') focusing on the scrap of paper that links four generations of the family.

- Tell the children that they are going to think about their own family stories, and any significant objects (talismans) that have been handed down through their family. Allow children time to choose either a family story (maybe about a relative living or from the past) or a significant object that has been passed down. Provide them with photocopiable page 36 'Stories and talismans' to fill in. Suggest that, if they prefer, they can imagine a story or object which might be passed down through a family, and describe why and how it became important.

- When they have finished, bring the class together and invite volunteers to summarise their family story or describe their lucky or significant object. Encourage children to say how they feel about that story or object, and let others ask questions and volunteer shared feelings or similar stories/objects.

Differentiation
Support: Prompt ideas with suggestions: a story about a family holiday, a relative or ancestor, an object owned by grandparents and so on.

Extension: Let children write up their family story or a description of a significant object.

6. In Flanders Fields

Objective
To articulate and justify answers, arguments and opinions.

What you need
Copies of *Poppy Field*, photocopiable page 37 'In Flanders Fields'.

Cross-curricular link
History

What to do:

- Tell the children that they are going to focus on the poem by John McCrae, 'In Flanders Fields', that features in the story. Look together at the full-page version of the whole poem that appears after the story. Ask a volunteer or volunteers to read it aloud. Encourage children to offer their own opinions and responses to the poem.

- Tell them that there are differing accounts of when the poem was written. One says that the poet was seen writing the poem the day after his friend Alexis Helmer died. This account says he was sitting on the rear step of an ambulance, looking at Helmer's grave and the poppies that were growing wild on the graves in the burial ground. Another account says he wrote the poem after Helmer's burial, and a third that he drafted it to pass the time waiting for wounded soldiers to arrive at his first-aid post. Ask: *Which version is the Poppy Field story closest to?* (the first)

- Hand out photocopiable page 37 'In Flanders Fields' and tell the children to fill it in, working in pairs. When they have finished, bring the class back together to share their ideas.

Differentiation
Support: Together, read through the poem line by line, checking that children understand the meaning.

Extension: Encourage the children to explore and discuss other First World War poems by Siegfried Sassoon, Wilfred Owen or Rudyard Kipling.

Why wear a poppy?

• Explain the significance of wearing poppies by completing the sentences below.

Poppies are a symbol of:

_____

Poppies are worn for three main purposes:

1. To honour _____

_____

_____

2. To raise awareness of _____

_____

_____

3. As a sign of _____

_____

_____

I would/wouldn't wear a poppy because _____

_____

_____

_____

Stories and talismans

• Think of a favourite family story or object and complete the sentence.

In my family, we have a favourite _____

_____

_____

Now briefly retell your story or describe the object.

_____

_____

_____

_____

_____

_____

Explain its importance to you and your family.

_____

_____

_____

_____

Explain how you feel about your family story and/or significant object.

_____

_____

_____

_____

In Flanders Fields

- Reread the poem 'In Flanders Fields' by John McCrae and answer these questions.

Who wrote the poem and why?

_____

_____

_____

_____

_____

Who is speaking the words of the verses?

_____

_____

How would you describe the mood of the poem?

_____

_____

What did the dead soldiers enjoy when they were living?

_____

_____

Note any examples of figurative language (such as alliteration).

_____

_____

_____

How does the poem make you feel?

_____

_____

_____

_____

GET WRITING ▶

1. Marie's diary

> **Objective**
> To use similar writing as models for their own.
>
> **What you need**
> Copies of *Poppy Field*, photocopiable page 41 'Marie's diary'.

What to do

- Read together from 'It was springtime, the spring of 1915' as far as 'and then hung the poem up on the wall'. Explain that they are going to draft Marie's diary entry about that day. Briefly revise the key features of diary writing (first person, past tense, informal style) and refer to any novels in diary form the children may be familiar with (such as *Diary of a Wimpy Kid*).

- Ask them to summarise the main events in Marie's day (walking up to the Field Hospital, picking poppies, spotting the soldier, her father framing and hanging the poem).

- Challenge them to suggest other things that Marie would do in the day, referring back to the text (collecting eggs or helping to milk the cows) and encourage them to think how she feels (enjoying her walk, being surprised that the soldier spoke to her in Flemish, seeing her father cry).

- Hand out photocopiable page 41 'Marie's diary'. Ask the children to complete it, referring back to the text for detail, before writing their draft diary entries. Remind them to write in the first person.

- Share diary entries as a class and decide which are the most convincing and why.

> **Differentiation**
> **Support:** List the main events in the day on the board for children to refer to.
> **Extension:** Children write a diary entry for another day, such as the day Marie met Piet.

2. One morning

> **Objective**
> To draft and write by composing and rehearsing sentences orally (including dialogue).
>
> **What you need**
> Copies of *Poppy Field*, examples of playscripts.
>
> **Cross-curricular link**
> Drama

What to do

- Tell the children that they are going to draft a short playscript. The scene should focus on Emile arriving home after he sees the vision of soldiers meeting during the Christmas truce.

- They need to write parts for three characters: Emile, Mama and Grandpa.

- Arrange the children into groups of three. Briefly revise the form of a playscript, referring to examples or modelling lines of dialogue on the board.

- Encourage the children to use words and information from the novel to help make their play script convincing. They could begin with the lines:

  Mama: Come and have some breakfast, Emile.

  Emile (sits down at the kitchen table): I've just been down to Poppy Field.

  Grandpa: Has the mist cleared?

- Ask them to discuss how Mama and Grandpa might respond to what Emile tells them. Ask: *Would they believe him?* Allow them time to discuss and rehearse their playscripts.

- Invite groups to present their playscripts to the class, discussing which are most effective and why.

> **Differentiation**
> **Support:** Begin the playscript on the board as a shared activity, then let pairs develop it.
> **Extension:** Pairs could draft another short scene, perhaps when Marie comes home to her parents and shows them the scrap of paper.

3. Poppy girl

Objective
To perform their own compositions, using appropriate intonation and volume so that meaning is clear.

What you need
Copies of *Poppy Field*.

What to do

- Begin by re-reading a verse from 'In Flanders Fields', first quickly and in a monotone voice, and then using tone and volume to express feeling. Ask: *Which reading was the most powerful?* Discuss how meaning can be emphasised using the voice.

- Tell the children they are going to plan, draft and read aloud their own poem about Marie, called 'The Little Poppy Girl'. Together, come up with some initial ideas about Marie and the poppies, making brief notes on the board.

- Arrange children to work in pairs to plan their poems. Write questions on the board for them to discuss and make notes on: *Who will speak the words of your poem? (Marie or a British soldier?) What will the mood be? What does Marie like about poppies and why does she pick them? Can you think of any figurative language such as alliterative phrases or a simile/metaphor to describe Marie or the poppies? How do you want your readers to feel?*

- Let the children work in pairs to develop ideas, then either work in pairs or individually to draft their poems.

- Ask volunteers to read their poems aloud, reminding them to consider tone, volume and pace to express mood and feeling. Invite constructive feedback and criticism.

Differentiation

Support: As a class, scan the novel together for ideas and note them on the board. Let pairs draft a verse of a poem.
Extension: Children could write a poem about the Christmas truce.

4. A poet's letter

Objective
To select the appropriate form and use similar writing as models for their own.

What you need
Copies of *Poppy Field*, examples of letters.

Cross-curricular link
History

What to do

- Tell the children that they are going to draft a letter that the poet in the story, John McCrae, might write to his family or a friend from the battlefields of Flanders.

- Before they begin, briefly revise the conventions of informal letter writing, looking at examples and modelling layout on the board.

- Discuss and list some things the poet might say in his letter. Suggest that he might tell them about writing his poem and describe the little poppy girl he meets, as well as telling them about the war and the death of his friend, Alexis. He might also ask how things are back at home.

- Arrange the children into pairs and ask them to discuss and note some ideas for the letter. They should decide who the poet is writing to back home in Canada (a parent, a brother or sister, a friend?) They should also try to imagine what else he might tell them – perhaps something about his work, and the wounded soldiers he has helped at his ambulance station.

- Ask individuals to then develop their notes into a draft of a letter.

Differentiation

Support: List ideas on the board as a shared activity then challenge pairs to draft a letter.
Extension: Let children use online resources to research letters sent home from the First World War battlefields.

5. A remembrance tour

Objective
To note and develop initial ideas, drawing on reading and research where necessary.

What you need
Copies of *Poppy Field*, completed photocopiable page 'Martens's home', access to the internet, photocopiable page 42 'A remembrance tour'.

Cross-curricular links
Geography, history

What to do

- Begin the lesson by discussing why many people like to visit the battlefields, memorials and cemeteries of the First World War. Some want to honour a family member who fought and died in the war. Others have studied the history of the war and want to see the significant sites for themselves. Throughout the areas where the major battles were fought in north eastern France and West Flanders (in southern Belgium) are numerous memorials, museums, military cemeteries and battlefield remains. Many are public sites which are signposted and accessible to visitors.

- Tell the children that they are going to plan a visitors' guide for people to tour the area around Poperinge in Flanders, where Martens lives.

- Arrange the children into pairs and provide photocopiable page 42 'A remembrance tour'. Let them skim and scan the story for places to visit (such as Poperinge, the Menin Gate, Cloth Hall, Ypres). They can also refer back to their completed photocopiable sheet 'Martens's home' and research the battlefields and memorial sites on the internet. Encourage them to choose four places to focus on. Allow the children time to make notes before developing them into four paragraphs.

- Invite pairs to present their paragraphs to the class.

Differentiation
Support: Ask children to focus on one place to visit and write one paragraph.
Extension: Encourage children to extend their paragraphs into a leaflet, adding illustrations.

6. Great War glossary

Objectives
To use dictionaries to check the spelling and meaning of words; to investigate spelling and understand the spelling of some words needs to be learned specifically.

What you need
Copies of *Poppy Field*, dictionaries, thesauruses, photocopiable page 43 'Great War glossary'.

Cross-curricular link
History

What to do

- Tell the children that they are going to compile a glossary of First World War terms found in the novel that would help readers of the novel understand more about the history of the war.

- Arrange the class into pairs. Hand out photocopiable page 43 'Great War glossary' along with dictionaries. Explain that they should first complete the cloze activity by filling in missing letters to complete the words or phrases. They should try guessing them from memory first, then refer back to the novel if they need to find or check a word.

- When the children have completed the activity, they should discuss together what they think each word or phrase means and draft a brief explanation for their glossary.

- When they have finished, they should exchange their pages with another pair and use a dictionary or thesaurus to check and correct the spellings and meanings where necessary.

- Bring the class back together to review their glossaries, encouraging pairs to improve their definitions and make them as concise and accurate as possible.

Differentiation
Support: Pairs can complete the cloze activity then use a dictionary or thesaurus to help them, though they should draft their own definitions.
Extension: Let children extend their glossaries by adding more words or phrases which specifically relate to the First World War.

Marie's diary

- Plan an entry for Marie's diary on the day she meets the soldier.
- Use the headings below to make notes.

What she did in the morning	The date

Who she saw

What he said to her

What she did next

What happened when she got home

A remembrance tour

- Use this sheet to plan a remembrance tour around the area of Poperinge.
- Choose four places to visit and write notes on each one.

Place	What you will see there

Great War glossary

- Fill in the gaps in the following words and phrases.
- Write a brief explanation of each word for a glossary to help readers of the novel.

Word/phrase	Explanation
1. F_ _ LD _ _SPI_AL	
2. K_AK_ G_EA_C_AT	
3. N_ M_N'S L_N_	
4. SH_ _ _	
5. TO_M_ES	
6. TR_NC_ _S	
7. Y_R_ _	

ASSESSMENT ▶

1. The whole story

Objective
To use and punctuate direct speech.

What you need
Copies of *Poppy Field*.

What to do

- Together, read from '"You knew that poppy poem, didn't you?" he said' as far as '"It's for luck. You should touch it too." And he did.' Write the first few lines of dialogue on the board, discussing and circling the punctuation to remind children how to punctuate direct speech. Point out that there is a new paragraph every time the speaker changes.

- Look together at the sentence 'Sitting in a café with him…'. Tell the children that they are going to write a new section of dialogue between Marie and Piet in which she tells him the 'whole story' and he responds. It should end with Piet's question "you've still got it?"

- Arrange the children in pairs. Write a first line of dialogue on the board: '"It was one morning when I had gone up to the Field Hospital to sell our eggs," Marie explained.' Let children continue the dialogue, including Piet's responses. Discuss a few ideas before they begin: he might ask how old she was at the time, whose grave it was she put the poppies on, and so on. Remind them to check their punctuation.

- Invite pairs to read their dialogue to the class. Choose some of the best lines and write them on the board, checking that the correct punctuation has been used.

Differentiation

Support: Briefly, summarise 'the whole story' in note form on the board for children to convert into dialogue.

Extension: Children write another section of dialogue from the story, perhaps Emile describing the soldiers in the mist.

2. Novel themes

Objectives
To summarise ideas from more than one paragraph; to identify themes.

What you need
Copies of *Poppy Field*.

Cross-curricular links
PSHE, history

What to do

- Ask the children what they think are the main themes in the novel (poppies as a symbol of remembrance; the power of a poem; the healing of a war-torn land; family; hope). Write ideas on the board, prompting them with questions such as *Which ideas come up more than once in the story? What links the generations of Martens's family?*

- If the children have recently read any other novels that cover similar themes (for example, the First World War) invite comparisons, focusing on key features such as narrative and style. Encourage them to offer their subjective opinions by beginning their comparisons with 'I think this is more interesting/moving because…'.

- Invite children to choose the theme they think is most significant, or which has most impact on them. They should draft a short statement beginning 'I think *Poppy Field* is a novel about…' describing the theme and why they think it is important. (For example, 'I think *Poppy Field* is a story about the power of poetry because the poem is like a talisman for all four generations of the Merkels.')

- Invite volunteers to read out their statements, and encourage children to give feedback.

Differentiation

Support: Provide a list of key themes on the board for children to choose from.

Extension: Children construct mind maps showing main themes in the novel with notes about each.

3. A family at war

Objective
To give well-structured descriptions, explanations and narratives for different purposes, including for expressing feelings.

What you need
Copies of *Poppy Field*.

Cross-curricular links
History, mathematics

What to do

- Tell the children they are going to consider the way the author uses time to structure the story of *Poppy Field*. Begin by revising how much time passes during the Merkel family story. Let children refer to the novel, then ask a volunteer to give evidence, citing relevant dates in the text. (Marie is eight in 1914; Martens is 11 in 2016.)

- Ask the children to consider the events that take place during the family story. Write on the board the headings 'World events' and 'Family events'. Invite them to give examples of significant events that happen during the period covered in the story under each heading, for example, 'World events: The First World War (1914–18), The Second World War (1939–45)'; 'Family events: Marie meets Piet, Grandpa meets Kate, Emile is killed'.

- List ideas on the board. Invite the children to explain how the world events influence the family events. Use their discussion to observe understanding of the historical context of the novel, and the way the family story is structured around the two world wars.

Differentiation
Support: Provide prompt questions to start discussion: *How does Marie meet Piet? How and when is Emile killed?*
Extension: Encourage children to discuss (being sensitive to individual circumstances) how current world events have affected their own families.

4. Fact or fiction?

Objective
To note and develop initial ideas, drawing on reading and research where necessary.

What you need
Copies of *Poppy Field*, photocopiable page 47 'Fact or fiction?'

Cross-curricular link
History

What to do

- Remind the children how in *Poppy Field*, as in many of his other novels, Michael Morpurgo has combined historical fact with a fictional storyline. Refer back to earlier work, such as Extract 2, Shared reading. Tell them that they are going to consider in more detail how the author based elements of his story on historical fact.

- Hand out photocopiable page 47 'Fact or fiction?' The children should complete the page, working individually. Encourage them to use the afterword to check facts. They can then exchange their work with a writing partner to compare and discuss their answers.

- Bring the class back together and invite children to read aloud their answers. Encourage them to discuss other books by Michael Morpurgo which have historical settings, and where he has woven a fictional story around historical facts (for example, *Kensuke's Kingdom, Private Peaceful, War Horse, The Amazing Story of Adolphus Tips*). The discussion should show their understanding of the difference between historical fact as presented in non-fiction recounts or documentaries, and fictional stories which are set in historical settings.

Differentiation
Support: Children can complete the photocopiable sheet in pairs and compare and discuss their work with another pair.
Extension: Challenge children to extend the photocopiable sheet with further examples using the same pattern.

5. Martens's story

Objective
To select the appropriate form and use similar writing as models for their own.

What you need
Copies of *Poppy Field*.

What to do

- Begin by reviewing the way the author uses Martens's words – speaking to us directly in the first person – to open and close the story. Re-read together the closing paragraphs from 'And that's how Grandpa ends the story…'.

- Tell the children to use their knowledge of the story to plan a sequel to the novel. Check – through reference to familiar books or films – that the children understand the concept of a sequel. Their sequel should somehow link back to the First World War, continuing the theme of *Poppy Field*, but as Martens was born in 2005 his story will be set in current times.

- Explain that their sequel should continue the story down the generations by focusing on Martens and something that happens later in his life. Briefly discuss some possible events. Perhaps Martens might get to see the vision of the Christmas truce? Or perhaps he might discover some memorabilia or debris from the war on the farm, which becomes significant to the family?

- Allow the children time to plan their sequel before they write two or three opening paragraphs in Martens's words.

- Invite them to read aloud their paragraphs and explain what will happen in their stories, encouraging positive feedback.

Differentiation
Support: Discuss some possible storylines and make notes on the board for children to use.
Extension: Let children complete a draft of their sequel.

6. Spell it

Objectives
To investigate spelling and understand the spelling of some words needs to be learned specifically; to use relevant strategies to build their vocabulary.

What you need
Copies of *Poppy Field*.

What to do

- Tell the children that they are going to identify words which have tricky spellings in the novel. Arrange children into small groups and allocate each group one part of speech: proper noun, noun, adjective, verb. List examples on the board to ensure that the children can recognise their chosen part of speech: 'Ypres', 'Flanders' (proper noun); 'cemeteries' 'soldier' (noun); 'khaki', 'beautiful' (adjective); 'ploughing', 'swapped' (verb).

- Challenge each group to scan the story to find six words in their category which have tricky spellings. They should nominate a note taker to write down their words.

- When they have finished, the groups should nominate someone to read out their words. Other groups can compete against each other to write down the correct spellings. Write the words on the board so that children can check and correct their own answers.

- Bring the class back together and award points for the group with the most correct spellings. Invite suggestions for which words were the hardest to spell. Reflect that some words are not used in everyday speech and may need us to use devices to help memorise their spellings (such as sounding the silent letters in 'khaki' or 'plough').

Differentiation
Extension: Let groups search the novel for more tricky spellings in each category.

Fact or fiction?

• Explain how the author uses the following historical facts in the story.

Fact 1: There was a Field Hospital known as Essex Farm near Brielen.

In the story, _____

_____

Fact 2: John McCrae was a doctor who wrote his poem 'In Flanders Fields' in the battlefields.

In the story, the soldier-poet writes the poem sitting near

_____

_____

Fact 3: The soldier-poet John McCrae scribbled and crossed out the lines in the first draft of his poem.

In the story, _____

_____

_____

Fact 4: On Christmas Night of 1914, enemy soldiers crossed No Man's Land to meet and exchange gifts.

In the story, _____

_____

_____

Fact 5: Unexploded shells remained a danger after the First World War.

In the story, _____

_____

_____

SCHOLASTIC
READ&RESPOND

Available in this series:

Key Stage 1

FOR AGES 5–7
978-1407-18254-4

FOR AGES 5–7
978-1407-16053-5

FOR AGES 5–7
978-1407-14220-3

FOR AGES 5–7
978-1407-15875-4

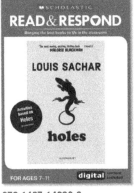

FOR AGES 5–7
978-1407-16058-0

Key Stage 2

FOR AGES 7–11
978-1407-14228-9

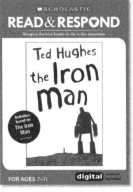

FOR AGES 7–11
978-1407-14224-1

FOR AGES 7–11
978-1407-14229-6

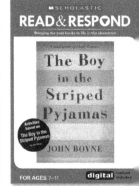

FOR AGES 7–11
978-14071-6057-3

FOR AGES 7–11
978-14071-6071-9

FOR AGES 7–11
978-14071-6069-6

FOR AGES 7–11
978-14071-6067-2

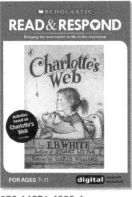

FOR AGES 7–11
978-14071-4231-9

FOR AGES 7–11
978-14071-4223-4

FOR AGES 7–11
978-14071-6060-3

FOR AGES 7–11
978-14071-5876-1

FOR AGES 7–11
978-14071-6068-9

FOR AGES 7–11
978-14071-6063-4

FOR AGES 7–11
978-1407-18253-7

FOR AGES 7–11
978-1407-18252-0

To find out more, call 0845 6039091
or visit our website www.scholastic.co.uk/readandrespond